LIFEWATCH

The Mystery of Nature

Bulb to Tulip

Oliver S. Owen

Published by Abdo & Daughters, 4940 Viking Drive, Suite 622, Edina, Minnesota 55435.

Printed in the United States.

Cover Photo credit: Peter Arnold, Inc.
Interior Photo credits: Peter Arnold, Inc. pages 4, 7, 8, 9, 10, 14, 16, 17, 19, 21, 25
Archive Photos, pages 11, 12, 15, 19, 23

Edited by Bob Italia

Library of Congress Cataloging-in-Publication Data

Owen, Oliver S., 1920
Bulb to tulip / Oliver S. Owen.
     p. cm. — (Lifewatch)
     Includes bibliographical references (p.28) and index.
     ISBN 1-56239-488-6
1. Tulips—Juvenile literature. [l. Tulips.] I. Title. II. Series:
Owen, Oliver S., 1920- Lifewatch.
SB413.T9094 1995
584'.324—dc20   95-8116
                                                          CIP
                                                          AC

Contents

Tulips

The tulip is a wonderful flower. It comes in a rainbow of colors, and often signals spring's arrival. Tulips had their beginnings in Turkey. Many years ago the Turkish sultan wore a turban—a scarf wound about his head. His turban was decorated with bright feathers and precious stones. Since tulips are bright and beautiful, and look somewhat like turbans, they were called "tulips" by the Dutch. ("Tulip" is the Dutch word for turban.)

Tulips come in a rainbow of colors.

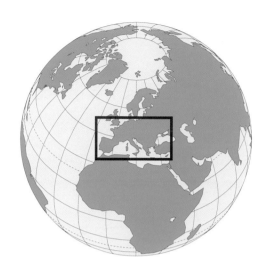

*Tulips had their beginnings in
the country of Turkey.*

Today, tulips are grown in gardens almost everywhere in the world. But it wasn't always that way. In the 1500s many kinds of beautiful tulips were sent from Constantinople, Turkey, to Vienna, Austria. From Vienna the tulips were shipped to flower lovers in other parts of Europe. In England and Holland the tulips became very popular. The tulip soon became Europe's most highly prized flower.

Between 1647 and 1650, the Dutch went wild over tulips. This tulip craze was called *tulipomania*. It became very fashionable to own a tulip garden. The cost of tulip seeds and bulbs went sky high. One Dutchman paid more than $5,200 for a single bulb of a variety called the Semper Augustus! The tulip industry was as important to Holland then as the car or computer industry is to the United States today.

The tulip craze made many Dutch businessmen very rich. Even today the tulip industry is big in the Netherlands (formerly Holland). It has produced thousands of varieties. The tulip is now the Netherlands' national flower. The city of Holland, Michigan, also has a big tulip business. As in the Netherlands, this town celebrates the tulip with a big festival every May when these flowers are in bloom. The people dress up in old Dutch costumes, sing, dance and have a great time.

The tulip industry
is very important
to Holland.

How the Tulip Plant Works

Seeds and Bulbs. Tulip flowers form small seeds you can plant in a flower garden. But it might take three to seven years before they develop into flowering plants. Instead of seeds, most people plant tulip bulbs. A tulip bulb is about two inches (five centimeters) long. It is somewhat rounded but has a "nose" on the upper end. It looks something like an onion. The bulbs help anchor the plants in the soil. Inside each bulb are all the main parts of the plant—roots, stem, leaves and flower. These

A tulip bulb.

parts are tiny. Tulip bulbs are planted in the fall. They stay alive throughout the winter. The energy the bulbs need is stored in their fleshy leaves.

Roots. Slender roots grow from the bulb into the ground. They help anchor the plant in the soil. Each root has millions of microscopic hairs. They take in water and nutrients from the soil.

Stem. Some tulip stems are only three inches (7.5 centimeters) long. Others are 30 inches (75 centimeters) long. Tulip stems have several jobs. They hold the plant in the air. This allows the leaves to take in and let out gases. The stem also holds the leaves in the sunshine so they can make food. The stem has pipelines which carry food from leaves to hungry parts of the plant, such as the roots and flowers. Other pipelines in the stem carry water and nutrients from the roots to the leaves.

The stem holds the plant in the air and allows the leaves to take in and let out gases.

Leaves. The strap-shaped leaves are the tulip's main food factories. To make this food, they take water from the soil. The water travels through the stem and into the leaves. Leaves also need carbon dioxide gas to make food. This gas passes from the air into the leaf through millions of microscopic breathing pores. The sun's energy powers the food-making act.

This energy is taken in by millions of tiny green wafer-like bodies called chloroplasts ("green bodies"). They contain a green pigment called chlorophyll ("green leaf"). The chloroplasts give the leaves their green color.

The strap-shaped leaves are the tulip's main food factories.

The food-making act in the leaf is called photosynthesis ("put together with light"). During photosynthesis, carbon dioxide and water are changed into energy-rich sugar. Then the plant burns the sugar to grow and reproduce (see page 13).

Flower. The flower has beautiful petals that delight the eyes of tulip lovers everywhere. But the flower also contains reproduction organs. The female organ is shaped like a long-necked vase. The wide lower part of the female organ is called the ovary. This is where the eggs are formed. The male organs, which are club-shaped, are known as stamens. Each stamen has a bag-like tip in which pollen is formed. For

The flower has beautiful petals that delight the eyes of tulip lovers everywhere.

reproduction to take place, pollen must touch the top of the female organ. This is known as pollination.

Pollination occurs with the help of insects. Many kinds of insects like beetles, ants and butterflies are attracted by the flower's bright colors or fragrant nectar. When the insect feeds on the nectar, dozens of tiny pollen grains dust its body. As the insect moves around in the flower, some of the pollen grains stick to the top of the reproduction organ. The pollen grain then forms a tube which grows down to the ovary. Then a "sperm cell" from the pollen grain moves down through this tube and unites with the egg in the ovary. This is called fertilization. This is how a seed is formed.

Tulip stamen.

The seeds are housed in a capsule. When they are ripe, the capsule splits open. Then the seeds fall to the ground. Inside each seed is an embryo or baby tulip plant. The following spring, the seed will grow into a tiny bulb.

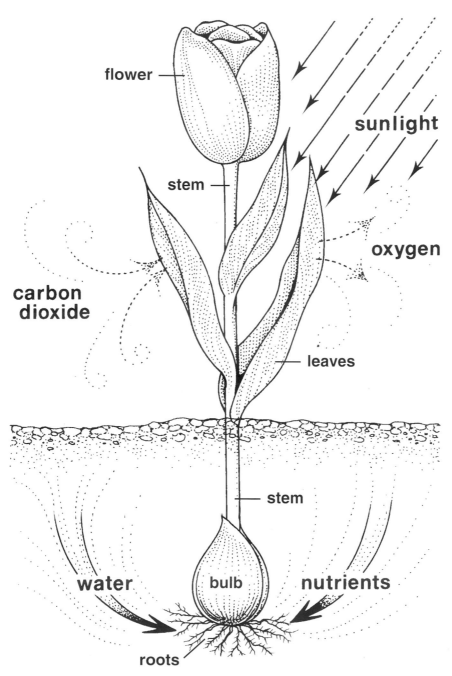

To make food, roots take in water and nutrients which travel through the stem and into the leaves. The leaves use sunlight and carbon dioxide to convert the water and nutrients into food. This is called photosynthesis. The leaves then release oxygen into the air.

The Kinds of Tulips

About 400 tulip species grow wild in Europe, Asia and Africa. However, many tulips are not very attractive. Some of the flowers are too small. Some are not brightly colored.

Gardeners have tried to make "improvements" on the wild tulips, known as varieties. More than 4,000 such varieties have been developed, most of them by the Dutch.

Roughly 400 tulip species grow wild in Europe, Asia and Africa. These tulips grow in Holland.

These tulips are brightly colored hybrids.

Sometimes two kinds of tulips are crossed to form hybrids. For example, a large, dull-colored tulip might be crossed with a small, brightly colored tulip. Such a cross might produce a large, brightly colored tulip which would be highly prized by flower lovers.

Some tulips have been developed which have two rows of petals, or have petals with fringed edges. Some varieties bloom for only about ten days. However, if a combination of early, middle and late spring varieties are planted, the gardener can enjoy tulips for a long time.

To have tulips blooming in your garden throughout May and June, plant nine varieties. In order of blooming, they are: Early Single, Early Double, Mendel, Triumph, Darwin, Lilly-flowered, Parrot, Breeder and Double Late.

The world's tulip industry is located mainly in the Netherlands, England, British Columbia and the United States. Over a billion bulbs are produced each year. Annual sales amount to more than $1 billion.

These tulips are from Skagit Valley, Washington.

Tulip varieties have some highly interesting names. Some were named after former kings, queens and princesses. Examples are Queen Wilhelmina, Queen of Bartigons, Queen of Sheba, Princess Margaret, Princess Beatrix, and Prince of Austria. A few varieties are named after important people.

Good examples are President Kennedy, General Eisenhower, General Montgomery, Cordell Hull (former Secretary of State), authors Shakespeare and Victor Hugo, artists Goya, Rembrandt and Van Gogh, composers Vivaldi and Cesar Franck, singer Perry Como, and violinist Frits Kreisler.

Many tulip varieties are named after important people, birds and colors.

Some tulip varieties are named after birds. Examples are Black Parrot, Blue Parrot, Peacock Hybrid, Black Swan, Blue Heron and Hummingbird. Most tulip varieties, however, are named after their colors. Examples include Blue Perfection, Gold Medal, Golden Harvest, Orange Bouquet, Sunkist, Bronze Charm, Pink Pearl, Pink Trophy, Ruby Red, Rose Mist, Peach Blossom, Apricot Beauty, Green Dragon, Silver Wedding, White Elephant, Snow Peak, Glacier, Moonlight, Sunburst, and Bonfire.

A tulip variety is often not just one solid color. The flowers of many varieties have a combination of several colors. The Cape Cod variety has petals which are orange-red and fringed with yellow on the outside, while the inside of the flower is bronze-yellow and striped with scarlet.

Viruses can affect tulips colors. Viruses usually cause diseases, both in plants and humans. But in some varieties the viruses are harmless. They may even increase the flower's beauty by adding lovely streaks of red, orange, yellow and silver to the petals.

The Greig Tulip is of special interest because its leaves are almost as beautiful as its flowers. The leaves are gray-green and spotted with dark purple. The flowers themselves are very large—about five inches (12.5 centimeters) across, and have a beautiful yellow center which is peppered with black spots.

A tulip variety is often not just one solid color.

Dangers to Tulips

Tulips are hardy plants. However, fungi can make them sick or die. One is the fungus Botrytis. A tiny, plump insect called an aphid infects the tulip with this fungus when it sucks sap from the leaves or stem. This fungus weakens the tulip and destroys its beauty.

Several kinds of animals will feed on tulips. Sometimes mice will gnaw at bulbs and stems. Rabbits will often make an early morning breakfast out of your tulip beds. Pocket gophers may burrow under the tulips and chew on the roots and bulbs. Slugs (snails without shells) will feed on stems and leaves.

Weather can also be highly destructive to tulips. If the bulbs are planted too shallow, a deep freeze will kill them. A big rain, hail or wind storm can flatten a tulip bed in minutes. Tulips will sicken and die if the soil lacks important nutrients. Even dense shade can be a killer. Tulip leaves need sunshine to make food.

Several kinds of animals will feed on tulips.

How to Plant a Tulip Garden

To plant a tulip garden, buy tulip bulbs from a garden store. If you want two colors—solid red and solid gold—the clerk might suggest the varieties "Ruby Red" and "Golden Melody." If you live in the Northern States, plant the bulbs in October. If you wait until November, cold weather might kill the bulbs.

Make sure your garden plot is well-drained. If pools of water form after a rainstorm, the tulips will drown and die. Before you plant the bulbs, loosen the soil with a hoe and rake it. A small amount of fertilizer might be added to the soil so the young tulip will get the nutrients it needs for good health and growth. Make sure you plant the bulbs with the nose down, at a depth of six to eight inches (15 to 20 cm), and six inches (15 cm) apart. If they are planted too shallow, the bulbs may be killed by heat or cold, or eaten by mice, squirrels and chipmunks. Press the bulbs gently into the soil with your fingers. It will take a few hours of hard work.

Tulip growers cutting tulip bulbs.

From Bulb to Tulip

Suppose you plant tulips. Though winter comes, the baby tulip plants inside the bulbs will stay alive. They will be protected from the cold by the six inches (15 cm) of soil which covers them. They'll live on the food which is stored in the scale-like leaves inside the bulbs.

As the months pass, the tiny tulip plant inside the bulb seems to be asleep. But in early April, the weather warms up and the baby tulip plant starts growing. The stem and leaves push upward through the soil. Roots grow downward from the bulb. Now the tulips grow fast, and can make their own food and green leaves.

By early May, the tulips are almost two feet (60 centimeters) high. Each plant has a big bud which is partly open. The next morning your big gold and giant-sized ruby red tulips have blossomed. Suddenly, all that hard work seems well worth the effort!

*Tulip hybrid,
Tokyo, Japan.*

Glossary

Aphid   tiny, plump insect that sucks fluids from plants.

Bulb   onion-shaped body containing the "baby" tulip; it is planted in fall.

Chlorophyll   green coloring in the plant leaf which makes food for the plant when the sun shines on it.

Chloroplast   microscopic body in the plant leaf which contains the chlorophyll.

Fungus   a group of plants which lack flowers, leaves or chlorophyll.

Ovary   the female organ of a flower in which the eggs are made.

Photosynthesis the process by which the green plant leaf makes food with the aid of energy from the sun.

Pollen dust-like grains made by the stamens which contain the "sperm cell."

Pollination the act by which the pollen passes from the stamens to the female organ of the flower.

Stamens the club-like male organs of the flower which make the "sperm cells."

Tulipomania a 17th Century craze during which tulips were in great demand in Holland and other parts of Europe.

Turban a scarf which is wound about the head.

Bibliography

Encyclopedia Americana. Entry on Tulips. Danbury, Conn.:
Grolier, 1994.

Hudak, Joseph. *Gardening with Perennials*. New York:
Quadrangle, 1976.

Snyder, Leon C. *Gardening in the Upper Midwest*.
Minneapolis: University of Minnesota Press, 1985.

World Book Encyclopedia. Entry on Tulips. Chicago Field
Enterprises, 1990.

Wright, Michael. *Garden Plants*. New York: Rainbird
Publishing, 1984.

Index

About the Author

Oliver S. Owen is a Professor Emeritus for the University of Wisconsin at Eau Claire. He is the coauthor of *Natural Resource Conservation: An Ecological Approach* (Macmillan, 1991). Dr. Owen has also authored *Eco-Solutions, Intro to Your Environment* (Abdo & Daughters, 1993), and the Lifewatch series (Abdo & Daughters, 1994). Dr. Owen has a Ph.D. in zoology from Cornell University.

To my grandson, Amati: May you grow up to always appreciate and love nature.
—Grandpa Ollie.